ALSO BY KATHLEEN BUCKSTAFF

The Tiffany Box, a memoir

A USA Best Book Awards Finalist

Mother Advice

To Take With You To College

text and illustrations

Copyright © 2014 by Kathleen Buckstaff

ISBN 978-0-9887-6425-5

Cataloging-in-Publication Data

has been applied for and may be obtained

from the Library of Congress.

Published by Two Dolphin Productions

San Francisco, CA

USA

CONTENTS

For my son.

When we said goodbye to you
in your dorm, I thought
my heart might break.

Even though we knew you were ready to go, Dad and I were still sad.

We bought a Kit Kat
and ate it on the way
home.
Chocolate helps.

But when I got home, I was still really sad.

There was so much
I wanted to tell you,
to make sure I told you...

I bought a notebook
and a pen. Whenever
I thought of something
I wanted you to know,
I wrote it down.

These words are
from my heart,
and they're for you.

A frisbee is a great way to meet new people.

Making a new, true
friend takes time.
Be patient.

Trust me. Clean sheets make everything better.

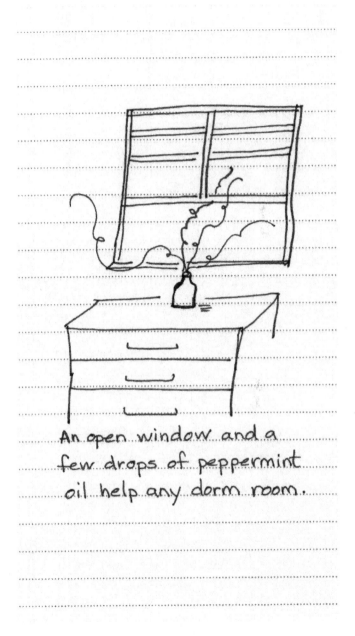

An open window and a few drops of peppermint oil help any dorm room.

Use shampoo when
you wash your hair.
Girls like clean hair.

```
      K
      N
          Y
P     O   O
L     W   U
E         R
A
S    Get to know your professors.
E   Most do crossword puzzles
    during office hours waiting
    for a student to come by
```

Get to know your professors. Most do crossword puzzles during office hours waiting for a student to come by

If you are feeling
stagnant, angry, bored,
tense, lonely, depressed...
→ exercise. ←
Exercise helps almost
everything.

When you have your first
birthday away from home,
remember:
1) You made my life when
   you came into it, and
2) Drink lots of water, too.

PUKE BUCKET

If you're puking a lot
from drinking a lot,
drink less.

If you and your friends have a really cool idea to do something super fun, and a little, tiny voice in your head says, "maybe not such a good idea"...

BREATHE,

and do something else.

The decision might save
your life.

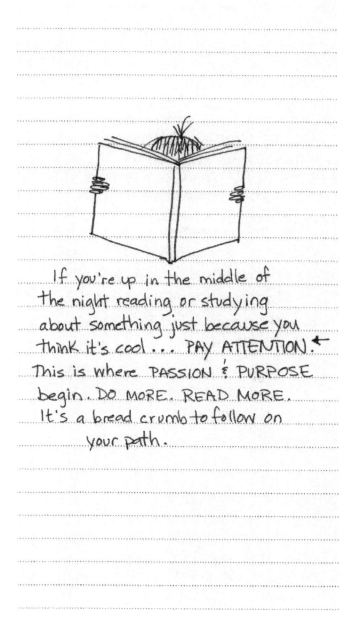

If you're up in the middle of
the night reading or studying
about something just because you
think it's cool ... PAY ATTENTION.←
This is where PASSION & PURPOSE
begin. DO MORE. READ MORE.
It's a bread crumb to follow on
        your path.

If none of your books or classes
are calling to you, ask yourself
the secret question. "Secretly,
I'd love to learn about _____."
And then go learn about it.
(Ignore the voices that say
too many other people are doing it,
it's stupid, or you'll never get a job.)

You can do hard things

When schoolwork gets tough, remember what your high school math teacher always said.

It's good to eat an apple before you take a test. Think of it as feeding your brain.

When you get sick,
drink 8 cups of
peppermint tea
a day and sleep more.

If you're sick and not getting better, go to the doctor. And I want you to remember when our dog was sick and I took him to the vet. When we got home, you asked me 100 questions. Did I ask the vet this? Did I tell the vet that?

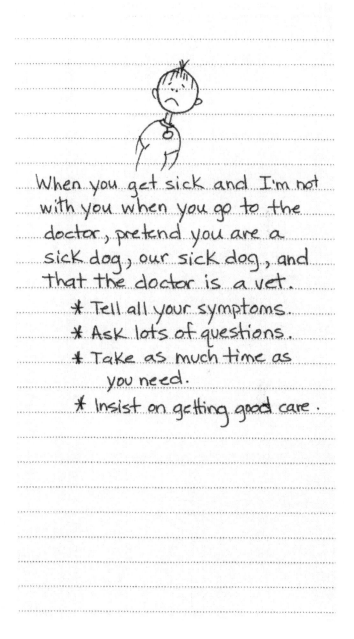

When you get sick and I'm not with you when you go to the doctor, pretend you are a sick dog, our sick dog, and that the doctor is a vet.

* Tell all your symptoms.
* Ask lots of questions.
* Take as much time as you need.
* Insist on getting good care.

I want to tell you a story.

When I was in college, I had a housemate. When he cut his own hair, he left all the hair in the sink.

When he ate cereal
every morning, he
left the milk out.

When he took showers,
he left wet towels
on the floor.

And he always left
the toilet seat up.

Remember, please remember,
to think of other people.

It's still important
to floss.

2

Use 2 forms of protection
every single time.

When you fall in love,
be kind to each other.

When you make a commitment
to be in a relationship with
another human, honor it.
        Be loyal.
Intimacy with another is
one of the best parts of life.
        Treasure it.
It is profound to love someone
        and to be loved.

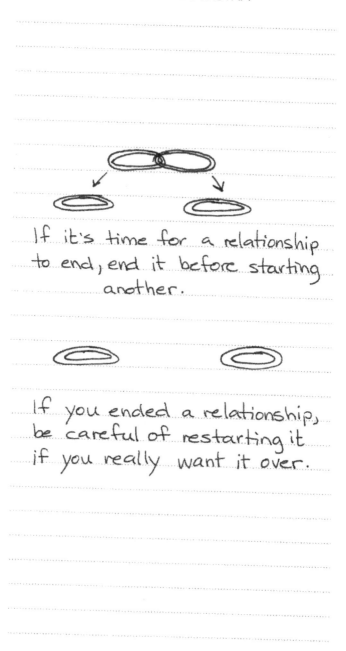

If it's time for a relationship
to end, end it before starting
another.

If you ended a relationship,
be careful of restarting it
if you really want it over.

When your heart
hurts, don't drive.
Lean against
a tree and she'll support you
and comfort you.

If you hear a bird singing,
stop and listen. The bird
is singing to you. Know that
and appreciate the song.

Make time to soak up
sunshine.

A Sanity Calendar ＊ ＊						
MON	TUES	WED	THURS	FRI	SAT	SUN
		1	2	3	4	5
6	7	＊8	9	10	11	12
13	14	15	16	17	18	19
20	21	22＊	23	24	25	26
27	28	29	30	31		

Set aside 1 hour
2 times a month
to deal with details:
pay bills, make appointments,
and contact people about
summer jobs.

When you were 6 and
your sister was 8½, you
had a lemonade sale.
Afterwards you two had a
big fight over who got how
much. Remember the lesson:
Have business conversations
early and often.
     Clear + upfront communications
reduce fights.

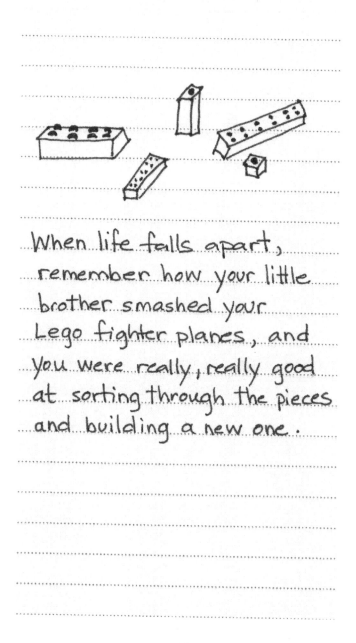

When life falls apart,
remember how your little
brother smashed your
Lego fighter planes, and
you were really, really good
at sorting through the pieces
and building a new one.

After you went backpacking
in yosemite, you told me
about walking through a
burned area. You told me
the forrest was charred +
black. You also told me that
when you looked closely, you
could see wild flowers growing.
You said flowers were the
first sign of new life.
Remember that.

Remember the shade of the
fig tree where you built forts,
ate pecans and tangerines.
It is a place of comfort for you
in your heart.

People can be jealous + cruel -
teachers, friends, coaches...
SHINE ANYWAYS!

Look at the moon
when you need
a moment of
peace and beauty.

On the night my mother
died, you were 7.
Every one else was crying, but
you looked up and said you
saw her and that she was
happy to not be in pain anymore.
You said she was sending
all of us love and that we'd
be with her again some day.

Remember when you convinced me to drive you to the top of a hill so you could skateboard down it and you hit a pot hole and had a gigantic wipeout? Remember how we laughed and laughed afterwards?

Laughter is the best medicine. (And crazy ideas spice up life — just make sure you survive them.)

If you are unsure what to do...
think from the end.

What do you want to do
with your one, beautiful,
precious life?

Try writing your own
obituary.

Remember the stand-up comedy routine you did in the kitchen. If you ever lose your sense of humor, fight with everything you have to get it back. It will save you.

When something good happens, celebrate!

After something good happens, actively work to remember the details about what was good.

*
It's important to focus on the good and build positive stamina.

Did you hear the story
about the college freshman
who didn't call his mother
on her birthday?
His mother cried, and his
father cancelled the
student's cell phone service.

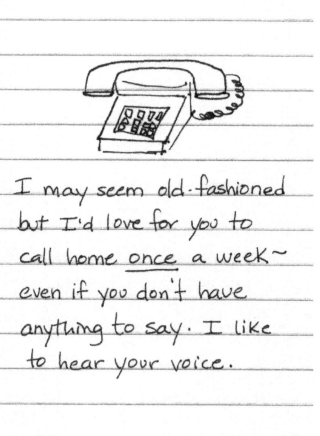

I may seem old-fashioned
but I'd love for you to
call home once a week ~
even if you don't have
anything to say. I like
to hear your voice.

When you come home
for breaks, I will
work on remembering
that you have been
on your own and that
you have changed.

Will you work on
understanding
that you will always,
always be
my son?

When you come home, will
you cook us a meal and
tell us stories?

I always love your stories,
and it will help remind me
that you've gotten older.

Hot dogs in a
pickle jar heated
in the microwave
don't count.

In my heart of hearts, ♡
I know God exists.
I also know God is loving
    and helpful.
You are never alone.
Even during your hardest
    times, grace moments
    will come.
Always be on the look-out
    for love + light + beauty.

When you don't know
what to do, say a
prayer and ask
for guidance.

When we went to the beach
for vacation, you loved riding
the biggest waves. Remember
that when you're considering
going for a dream that's
outside of your comfort zone.

DREAM BIG! ...

and then take
many tiny, little steps.
One at a time. If you start
feeling frustrated or afraid,
take a smaller step.

you were not sent
here to be like
everyone else.

It's important to remember
to fight for your life.
You're worth it.

As you grow up, Keep the
little boy in you alive - the
one who believed he could
launch a rocket to the moon.
The child inside
is where joy lives.

You have a unique & beautiful God Light inside of you.
Find it. Feel it.
Trust it. Share it.

Remember when
you stood up tall beside
the doorway — to show me
how tall you've gotten and
how much you've grown.

What you can't see
is how much I'm growing
as I watch you walk through it.

Here. Take it. It's my heart.
It's yours. I gave it to you
a long time ago — the day
you first smiled at me.
Wrap it around you, and _always_
remember this:
    You ARE LOVED!

A note to the reader ~

I am certain there is more essential advice to offer a child going off to college.

What did I forget ???

I will not be able to assign credit to you, but I may include suggestions in a future book.

Please email me at 2katbuckstaff@gmail.com. I'd love to hear from you.

XO

Kathleen

About the author:

Kathleen Buckstaff is the mother of three children. She lives in the San Francisco Bay Area with her husband in a nest that feels bigger these days. Her memoir on motherhood, The Tiffany Box, was a USA Best Book Awards Finalist. She writes regularly for The Huffington Post, and enjoys yoga and time with her lab puppy.

About The Tiffany Box, a memoir:

The Tiffany Box is full of love, humor, heartache, and insight. A gathering of emails and letters to her closest friends comprise Kathleen Buckstaff's candid, funny, and recognizably true chronicle of a generation "in-between": nurturing its young while nursing its aged, and coming to terms with the bitter realities that temper life's sweet rewards.

For students and parents, please feel free to use the next couple of pages to write your own advice. Enjoy!

....

....

....

....

....

....

....

....

....

....

....

....

MOTHER ADVICE

MOTHER ADVICE

....

....

....

....

....

....

....

....

....

....

....

....

....

....

Made in the USA
San Bernardino, CA
25 September 2015